Whatever You Are Be A Good One

Inspirational Coloring Book for Adults

I BELONG TO:

_____

_____

Thank you for your purchase!

Dear valued customer,

We hope you will enjoy our book!

Please consider leaving a review on Amazon. We would love to hear your feedback as we always trying to create better and better books.

We read every one of your thoughtful messages, and reviews are the best way to let other potential customers know about the book.

We are forever grateful to you!

Want free goodies?
Write the title of your purchase
as the subject of the email
Email us at:
genestudio01@gmail.com

QUESTIONS & CUSTOMER SERVICE?
Email us at:
genestudio01@gmail.com

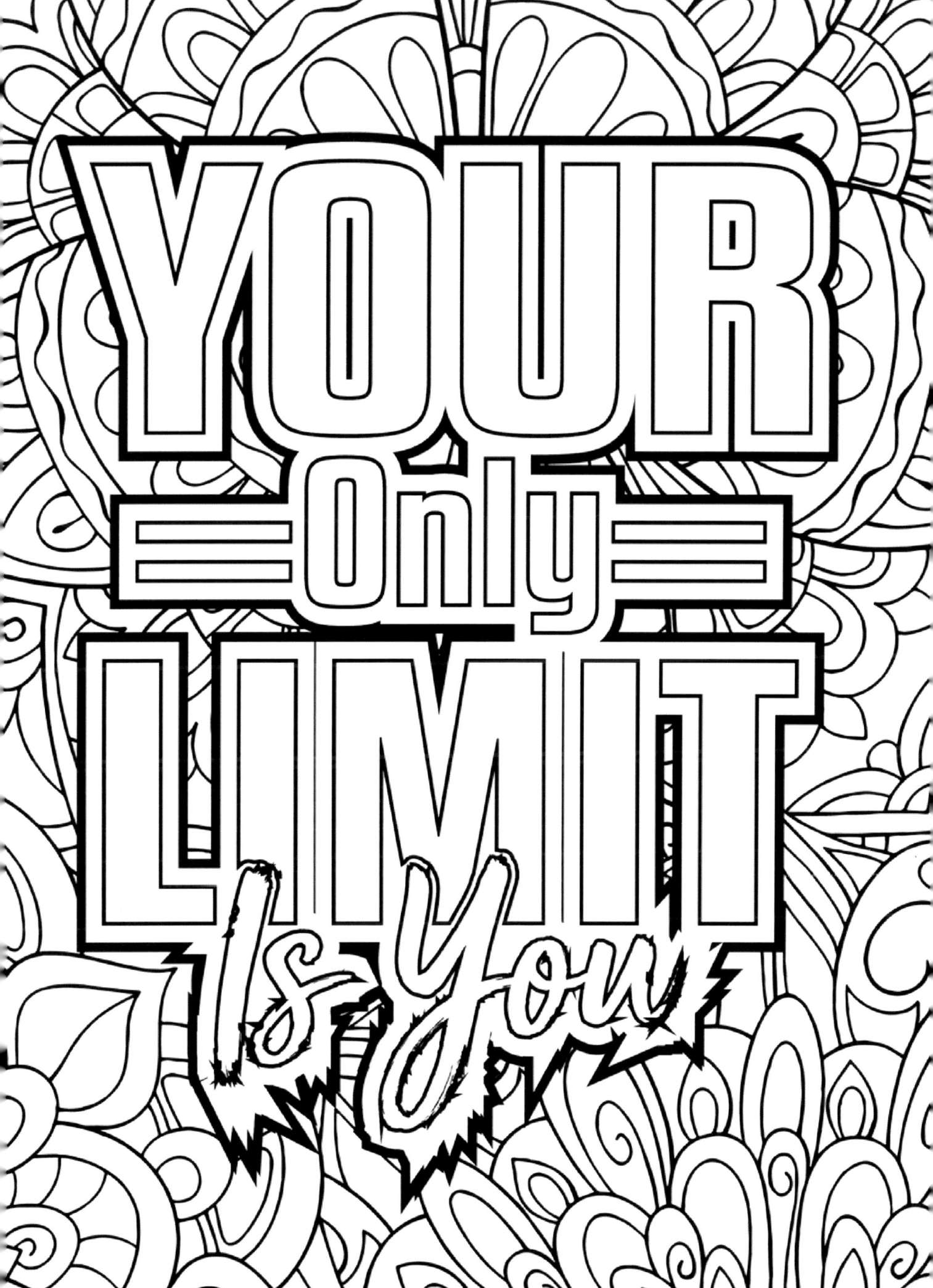

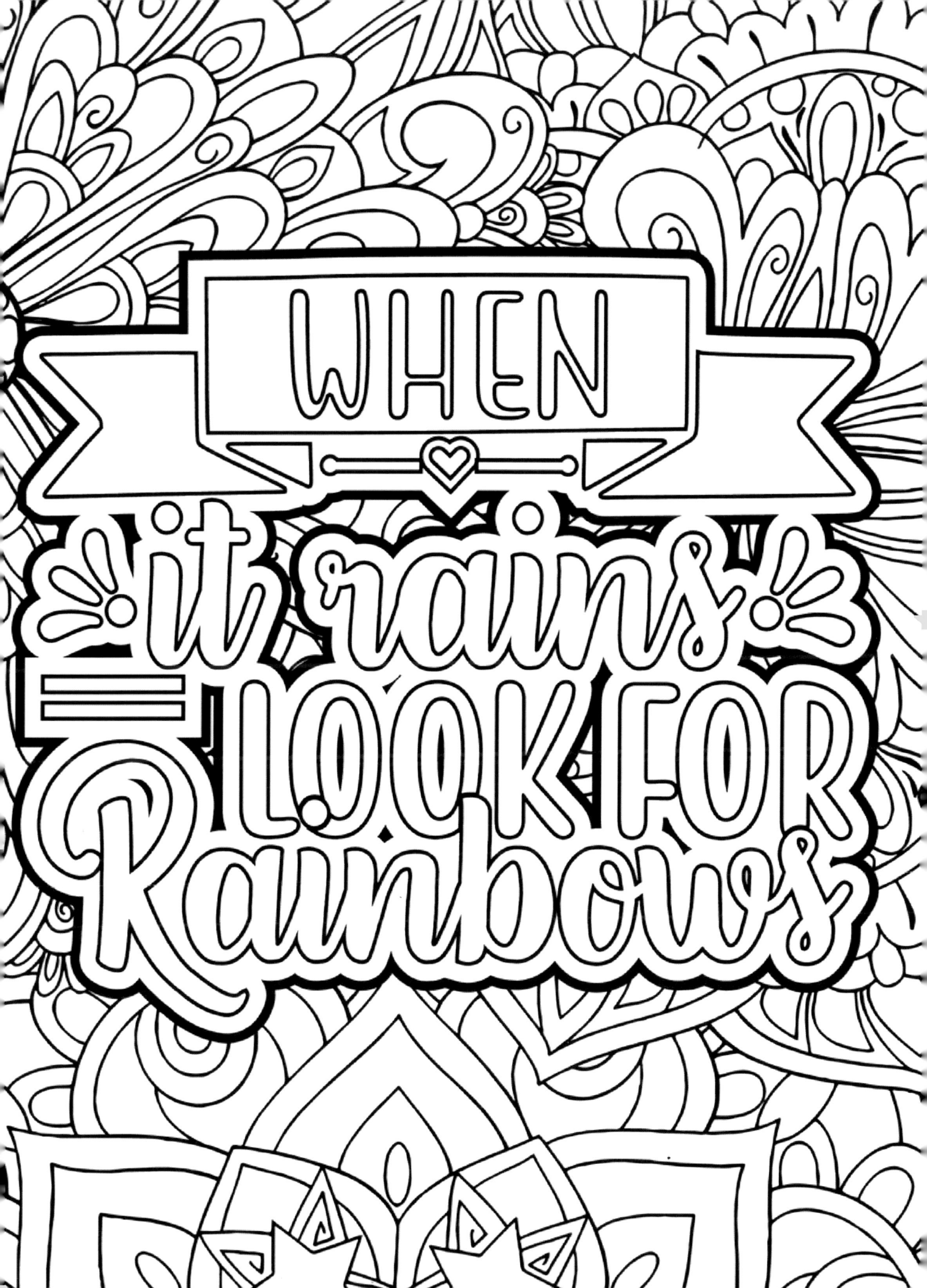

Dear valued customer,
If you like our book, please consider taking a look at the other books for adults

Link Here

 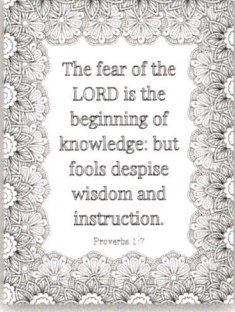 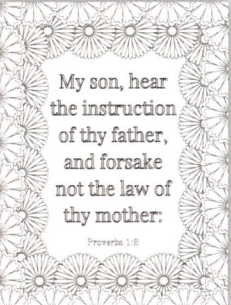 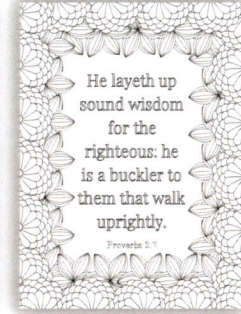 

Link Here

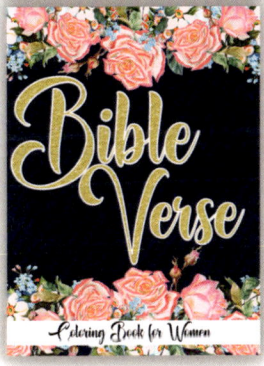 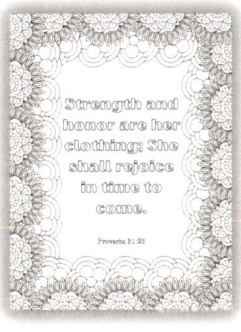 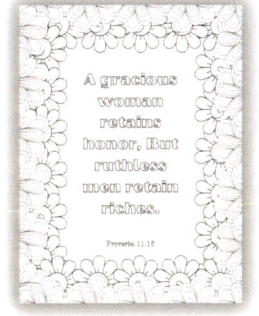 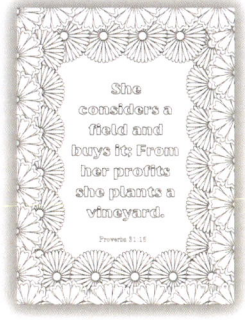 

Link Here

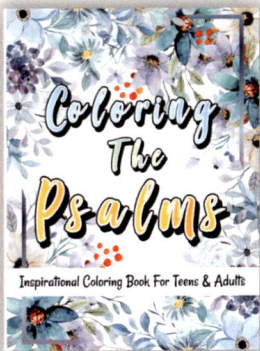    

Link Here

Thank You for your purchase!

© **Copyright 2022 - All rights reserved.**

You may not reproduce, duplicate or send the contents of this book without direct written permission from the author. You cannot hereby despite any circumstance blame the publisher or hold him or her to legal responsibility for any reparation, compensations, or monetary forfeiture owing to the information included herein, either in a direct or an indirect way.

Legal Notice: This book has copyright protection. You can use the book for personal purpose. You should not sell, use, alter, distribute, quote, take excerpts or paraphrase in part or whole the material contained in this book without obtaining the permission of the author first.

Disclaimer Notice: You must take note that the information in this document is for casual reading and entertainment purposes only. We have made every attempt to provide accurate, up to date and reliable information. We do not express or imply guarantees of any kind. The persons who read admit that the writer is not occupied in giving legal, financial, medical or other advice. We put this book content by sourcing various places.

Please consult a licensed professional before you try any techniques shown in this book. By going through this document, the book lover comes to an agreement that under no situation is the author accountable for any forfeiture, direct or indirect, which they may incur because of the use of material contained in this document, including, but not limited to, — errors, omissions, or inaccuracies.

www.ingramcontent.com/pod-product-compliance
Lightning Source LLC
Chambersburg PA
CBRC100222100526
44590CB00008B/144